Mindful
Kindful

**BOOK ZERO : AN INTRODUCTION TO
PRACTICAL MINDFULNESS**

Tom Evans

Tmesis Ltd

Surrey UK

Mindful Timeful Kindful

An Introduction to Practical Mindfulness

Practical Mindfulness Book Zero

ISBN : 978-1-849148474

Disclaimer

The purpose of this book is to educate and entertain. The author and publisher of this book do not dispense medical or psychological advice. You should not use the techniques herein for treatment of any physical or medical issues without seeking the advice of a qualified medical practitioner.

In the event you use any advice from this book, the author and publisher assume no responsibility for your actions.

Image credits

Contents

to Louise for all your kindfulnesses

Fore Words

WELCOME TO THIS INTRODUCTORY BOOK IN THIS SERIES ON PRACTICAL MINDFULNESS.

This book is intentionally short, as it is introductory in nature.

This first book in the series explores not only the state, and purpose, of mindfulness but also the practices of both timefulness and kindfulness.

Mindfulness seems to be in vogue these days, and this is a Good Thing. As an ex-engineer, I became intrigued with how the practice of mindfulness could deliver real-world, practical outputs. This transforms mindfulness from a nice and relaxing thing to do, which it is, to becoming a smart and efficient way to be.

We can use mindfulness to become not only more vital and healthy but also more creative and productive.

I refer to this state as 'timefulness', which we enter into naturally from the regular practice of mindfulness.

In this state, we get more done, of higher quality, in less time. In addition, external events seem to occur just when we need them. Rather like the idea for this book and series.

We are then led to a new strategy called 'kindfulness' which is our expression and reflection of our mindfulness back to the world. As you will see, it starts by being kind to ourselves. When we are in this loving state, it is easy to radiate out kindnesses to others and the planet, as a whole. This, of course, sets up a beautiful loop where the Universe bestows unlimited kindnesses back to us.

So Mindful, Timeful, and Kindful is a Way to Be. It is agnostic, yet embracing of all creeds and faiths. It also embraces and encourages a mindful type of hedonism that is ecological and ethical, and not to the detriment of others.

Being Mindful, Timeful, and Kindful opens the door to a simpler, richer, more rewarding and stress-free life. It is not a cult with any dogma to follow or leader to worship. It is also 'nicely infectious'. When others see good fortune come your way, they will want to know the secret. You will look more radiant and attractive—in all senses—and people may ask if you have had some sort of 'treatment'.

Just imagine having more time to do what you want to do just when you want to do it. Imagine a life that is bristling with positivity, creativity, invention and innovation. Imagine always having enough money coming your way, just when you need it.

This series of books even explores how creativity and revenue generation can occur while you are sleeping.

This may sound like a utopian pipe dream. I would not and could not make such claims and write this book if I had not experienced this way of life myself and helped many others achieve it too.

My overarching philosophy is to help make the world a better place to live in, and on. In some respects, my motive might be somewhat selfish. I have to live on this Spaceship Earth too and am fed up to the back teeth of seeing so much hatred, cruelty, greed, and wanton destruction around. It fills our news channels, and good news stories rarely get a look in. If you have the merest suspicion that we might reincarnate, it makes sense to leave the planet in a better state than how you found it—just in case you have to come back and do it all again.

This is potentially a century of true enlightenment. Now that we can see our planet from space and realise how special, and possibly unique, it is in the cosmos, it is time we changed our role from mere users of the planet to being its guardians and custodians. We have a duty that extends beyond the human species too. The whole biomass is required to sustain the food chain, for all creatures. The planet herself has needs, awareness, and feeling too. To live a truly mindful existence, the sky is not the limit—indeed there are no limits.

Dream on and dream up.

Why Book Zero?

YOU MAY WELL WONDER WHY IT IS CALLED BOOK ZERO RATHER THAN BOOK ONE.

This, of course, is intentional, as it is, of course, mindful.

Everything you see around you came from nothing—or 'no-thing'. What's more, only 0.000001% of the world around us is what we can call matter. This means the world around us is 99.99999% 'no-thing'. This massive percentage of 'stuff' is actually potential. It contains the potential to create the 0.000001% of everything we see.

Note that this percentage keeps getting revised down and it may be just 0.000000001%, or even less.

Our minds hold the key to tap into this potential, and the practice of mindfulness is what opens the door. Practical mindfulness creates a whole new world of potential and possibilities.

It is alchemy in action.

- Our minds create the world that we notice.
- Our minds are capable of altering the speed of time.
- Our minds are time machines and can visit the past and 'see' the future.
- Our minds can influence both organic and inorganic matter.
- Our minds are capable of imagining and realising a new world.
- Our minds are now capable of influencing our evolution.

Each of us is a channel, an oracle, and a healer. We just have to tap into our inner gifts, and they will appear—as if by magic.

Practical mindfulness is the key. Realising that every 'thing' comes from 'no-thing' is what opens the door.

Part 1

What is Mindfulness?

THE WHOLE WORLD SEEMS TO HAVE WOKEN UP TO MINDFULNESS THESE DAYS. COMPANIES, SCHOOLS, AND EVEN GOVERNMENTS ARE EMBRACING IT AND EXTOLLING ITS BENEFITS.

There is, perhaps, some confusion that mindfulness means meditation—and that meditation means mindfulness. Let me state from the outset, you can be mindful without meditating and meditate without being mindful.

This confusion is, perhaps, understandable, as learning to meditate is the most common route to achieving a mindful state of being.

As mindfulness has its roots in Buddhist philosophy, it is natural that meditation plays such a big role.

To confuse things a little further, though, one of the meditative techniques used to teach mindfulness is to empty the mind of all thought. So, in some respects, being 'mind-full' involves being somewhat 'mind-less'.

The words 'mindless' and 'mindlessness', though, bring up all sorts of connotations we want to avoid.

A better term all round would be that of 'mind-emptiness'. By emptying our minds of such mental clutter that creates 'a barrage of noise' in our heads, we are able to bring in a new quality of thought entirely.

To clear such potential confusion up before we get going, let's deconstruct the word 'mindfulness' into its constituent syllables of 'mind', 'full', and 'ness'.

In reverse order, 'ness' is a suffix that can be added to a word to make the root word refer to action, quality, or state.

'Full' implies something is brimming or even overflowing.

These two syllables can then be added to a root word, like 'mind', such that 'mindfulness' means a mind that is full and complete, leading to new action, increased quality, and a higher state.

The 'mind' referred to in this context is not the model of a mind somehow generated by our brains.

For starters, and as you will see throughout this series, we have mind centres all over our body that 'talk' in different languages and manners—and at different times, too. We are all connected by a collective mind that sits outside time and space. Being mindful of the nature of mind is an important part of the journey.

This universal concept of mind is nothing new and has been known about by mystics and sages for thousands of years. Only now are we starting to grasp the multidimensional physics that supports this model of mind, and we now possess MRI scanners that can detect activity in our whole neurology. By studying our inner space, we become able to understand our place in the 'outer space' we call reality.

As I mentioned, this introductory book extends the concept of 'mind-full-ness' to use the words 'time' or 'kind' in order to create the new words 'timefulness' and 'kindfulness'. I hope you can see already that these two pseudo-words have the potentiality to lead us to a new way of being and doing.

When we are 'full of time', we get loads done, and events happen around and for us at just the perfect time. When we are 'full of kindness', we are good to the world and the world is good to us in return.

So, while meditation can help us achieve the state of mindfulness, mindfulness is a Way to Be and a strategy we can use to have a happy and fulfilling life.

It is through the practice of 'mindfulness meditation' that we achieve the state of mindfulness.

Practical mindfulness is then how we use mindfulness techniques for real-world outcomes.

Mind-less-ness, and mind-emptiness, are the precursors to mind-full-ness.

My Mindful Journey

I DISCOVERED THE WORLD OF MEDITATION AND MINDFULNESS BY ACCIDENT.

In fact, the actual term mindfulness only entered my awareness a few years ago when everyone seemed to be using it.

In my mid-forties, like many people at that age, I felt disillusioned, stressed out with corporate life, and pondered the meaning of life in general. I met someone who suggested I should meditate because I looked haggard. My initial reaction was that I was too busy to waste ten or twenty minutes each day and that I could in no way make my mind go quiet.

I persisted though and discovered some simple ways to quieten my mind with breathing techniques. What happened over the following year changed my world.

I discovered that the days when I didn't meditate in the morning didn't go smoothly. It was like getting out of bed on the wrong side.

On the days when I did take the time to meditate, I found I got so much more done, and all the ducks would line up in a row. I got the time invested back in spades.

The real shift came when I learned how to stay in the meditative state with my eyes open. I found that my creativity and productivity shot up even more. I also learned how to channel, which is the subject of one of the books in this series.

I had simply been unaware that from when we awaken until when we fall asleep, our mind chatters away. It runs a commentary on what is going on around us; it rehearses things we are planning to say; it replays things we said yesterday. It is also capable of flights of imagination by creating pictures, soundscapes, and stories.

The fact that three pounds of matter can do this is nothing short of miraculous. These thoughts that run around in our head dictate the type of world we inhabit. If our thoughts are positive and optimistic, we will live in a kind world. If our thoughts make us depressed, angry, fearful, or sad, we will live in a world out to get us. If our thoughts are creative in nature, we will influence the world around us with our arts and our deeds. If we become masters of thought, we will learn how thoughts don't just become things but that they are things.

I discovered that it is possible to influence the world around us with thought alone.

It is also as easy to tap into 'future memories' as it is ones that have passed us by.

Adoption of a mindful outlook and practice is the key to performing such magical feats. If we meditate first thing every morning, it helps us control the flow of our thoughts so that they don't rage into a torrent. This becomes especially useful when we control and direct our thoughts in both a timeful and kindful manner.

It is well documented, and perhaps no surprise then, that the main benefit we get from mindful meditation is reduced stress. This in turn fosters improved health and general well-being. When we are healthier, we become more vital and creative and productive. All of this can come from the practice of taking 10 — 20 minutes of 'me time' every day.

If your work or family makes this difficult first thing in the morning, you can meditate at a lunchtime. If meditation time is impossible, just going for a walk in a park is a good substitute.

Where everything goes up a gear or three is when mindfulness is used for practical, so-called real-world outputs. The state of our consciousness, and the nature of our thoughts, control the subjective passage of time. When we take our thoughts under control, we can change the speed at which time passes, so we get more done with less of it.

When we understand the true nature and source of our thoughts, we can tap into ideas and innovation on demand.

When we tune into other mind centres inside our body, we can learn how never to put a foot wrong and how always to make the right decisions.

This, in turn, all saves us bags of time.

Why People Don't Meditate

There are numerous reasons people don't meditate. Here are some of the most common I come across.

1. You don't have the time

Meditation reduces stress and makes us less prone to illness, so any time spent comes back many times over by reducing time spent off work.

2. You can't make your mind go quiet

Meditation is not so much about having no thoughts at all as it is about forming a different relationship with them. When we are kinder to our thoughts, they are kinder to us. As thoughts become things, it pays dividends to have the good ones.

3. You have to be in a quiet room

We can meditate when out walking, when commuting, or even when washing the dishes or mowing the lawn. It is easy to integrate meditative practices into what we think of as our busy lives.

4. You have to have your eyes closed

If you ever drive home on 'autopilot' on a familiar route, you have entered a light meditative state. We are all natural meditators.

5. It will take years of study

Learning to meditate is easy. It only takes ten minutes a day for around a week to get the hang of it.

6. You have to study with a master

Put 'free meditation' into Google and get your 'master' to come to you.

7. It conflicts with your religious beliefs

Meditation is agnostic. Reciting of prayers, or repeating learned responses to a celebrant, actually induces a light state of meditation.

8. It's dangerous, and you might lose control of your mind

The person who is meditating remains in control at all times. In the same way nobody else can breathe for you, nobody else can meditate for you.

9. There are no practical benefits

Lightbulb moments come to us when we enter the meditative state. Your next bright idea is just one meditation away. Time stretches when we enter the meditative state with our eyes open. This allows us to get more done in less time.

Knowns and Unknowns

SCIENTISTS, NEUROLOGISTS, AND EVEN CLINICIANS ARE NOW STUDYING THE BENEFITS OF MEDITATION.

By using MRI scanners and looking at the brains, they can make great leaps forward in understanding the overall neurology of meditators.

What is emerging is astounding:

- Meditation reduces pain and inflammation
- Meditation reduces stress and anxiety
- Meditation delays the onset of degenerative mental illness
- Meditation helps overcome addiction
- Meditation improves digestion and reduces bowel irritation
- Meditation reduces blood pressure
- Meditation increases fertility
- Meditation improves the immune system and bone density
- Meditation gives better tonality to the skin

- Meditators think faster and have faster reaction times
- Meditators notice more of what is going on around them
- Meditators have improved recall and memory

Further study and acceptance will lead to meditation becoming commonly integrated into education, within our home life, and in the workplace.

What Has Yet to Be Understood

It is such a breath of fresh air that meditation is being actively researched and embraced by the scientific and medical communities. It is, perhaps, obvious that meditation techniques that increase and improve the breath also help reduce blood pressure and create improvements at a cellular level.

What is, perhaps, less appreciated are the benefits of meditation on reducing deleterious effects of unhealthy thoughts, especially the repetitive thought forms that cause dis-ease.

Consider this:

- Lack of love, and self-love, weakens the heart and impairs circulation
- Fears and phobias cause irritations in the bowel
- Fear of our mortality, or just boredom, can sow the seed for dementia
- Lack of self-worth and poor self-esteem make us prone to allergies and illnesses

More esoteric aspects of meditation not commonly understood or acknowledged are:

- Meditation removes our sense of 'separate-ness'
- Meditation tunes us into the collective mind
- Meditation increases our super-sensibilities
- Meditation changes our perception of time
- Meditation makes us 'luckier'
- Meditation makes us more 'attractive'—in life, love, and business
- Meditation reduces ageing—by slowing time down
- Meditation gives us the ability to heal others

Living Mindfully

AS I SAID, MEDITATION IS NOT MINDFULNESS, AND YOU CAN BE MINDFUL WITHOUT BEING IN THE MEDITATIVE STATE.

Practising daily meditation, especially first thing in the morning, is a great tonic to take in order to run your days mindfully.

So, what does a day spent mindfully entail? Here are nine simple ways to make your days go with a swing and a bounce:

1. Owning your thoughts

The purpose of mindfulness practice is to free ourselves from being enslaved by our thoughts.

This does not mean we become callous and unfeeling. From such a position of neutrality, we become a tower of strength when the world might be collapsing, or just difficult, for those around us.

So if a thought comes along that brings you down, or your mind moves in a direction that you find distracting, the simple step to take is to talk to that thought. Ask who sent it and what its purpose is. Ask it what you would have to do in order for it to go away and never come back.

If an inspiring thought comes your way, it's time to act. You can take that inspiration and do something with it right away, like writing it in a journal or notebook. If time doesn't allow, make a future date in your diary to meet with that inspiration again and to develop it into something in the 'real world'.

2. Managing your emotions

If anger, sadness, fear, guilt, or hurt comes our way, all thoughts of being mindful can go out of the window. Such emotions are generated outside our head in our lower mind centres. They can take over our mind and lead to thoughts of revenge, lack of self-worth, apathy, and hopelessness.

As for the 'verbal' thought forms in our head, we can tackle such emotional distractions with a mindful approach. Indeed, control of such emotions is one of the main benefits from the practice of mindfulness. As we can only have one thought at a time, if such thoughts take over our brain, our productivity suffers as a result. I call such raging emotions 'mindfalls'.

The way to escape from such a 'mindfall' is to ask the emotion what it is teaching you. What can you learn from it and your reaction to it?

Once the lesson is learned, the situation rarely comes back again. If it does, your reaction to it alters.

3. Managing your reactions

We can be having a great day when external events can take over our world. It might be something you see on the news, or someone in your family, or at work, that disrupts your day. Our plans to do what we planned to do can go out of the window if our thoughts get taken elsewhere, or if someone else puts demands on our time.

In these cases, we have two choices. Firstly, we can choose to ignore it and make time to deal with the situation later. Secondly, we can drop what we are doing and tackle what has caused the distraction. The key is to take either course of action mindfully.

So, either we can schedule a time to deal with it or reschedule what we are doing at the time to a later time or date. By responding to life events in such a mindful manner, we embrace life and avoid avoiding it.

4. Managing what you say

If you have ever said something that you regret, you will have experienced how your mind can create another kind of 'mindfall' where what we said replays incessantly in our minds.

We might think of better ways to have said it, or ways we can make amends for what we said. Such replays can play havoc with our efficiency and focus.

A simple way to avoid such 'faux pas' is to take a breather. Literally, before you start to say something or start a discussion, take one or more in and out breaths mindfully. This may either prevent us from saying the wrong thing or give us time to come up with an alternative way to express our thoughts and feelings.

5. Mindful Mails and Timeful Tweets

To live a truly mindful existence, we should be considerate about the manner in which we make an impact on the time of others. Every email you send, and every social media post, will take someone's time to respond to—as well as taking your time to compose. If people do respond and react to it, this will then take more of your time to read their response and perhaps reply to. With billions of emails, tweets and Facebook posts, you can see how we have created a cascade leading to a paucity of time.

To jump out of this temporal maze, all you have to do is to be mindful of everything you send or post, and when you do it. Ask yourself if it has to be sent now and be mindful that your time will be taken up by responding to it. Ask if there is a better way to say something. Be mindful of who you put in the 'cc' and 'Bcc' fields. If you tag people on Facebook or Twitter, ask yourself if they might mind being associated with your post.

6. Speaking your truth

If we are not allowed to say what we truly think, this too can lead us into a 'mindfall'. What we want to say, and how we plan to say it, can create self-talk that then repeats incessantly.

If we can't get a word in, for whatever reason, there are some simple ways to get things off your mind. Just write down, on paper or computer, what it is that you want to say, and file it away. If you have something big to say, not particularly directed at one person, write a blog or even a book.

If what you want to say is outrageous or just 'out there', use metaphors or fiction to get your point across. See any of my books for examples of my 'trojan horse' approach to getting metaphysics to a wider audience.

7. Noticing signs

If more than one person recommends a book, a TV programme, or a film to you, take heed. Often if a message is meant for us, the universe will find ways to repeat it so that we listen.

If we continue to ignore such assistance, the volume can get cranked up so that we do pay attention. So, if you are facing adversity in your life, especially if the same barriers keep appearing, it pays great dividends to spot the pattern and to break it. In many cases, just spotting such signs is enough to make the situation go away.

8. Being open to possibilities

If you remember that only 0.000001%, or less, of what we see is actual matter, that leaves much scope for potential. Repeated signs are one manifestation and reminder that there is another way. Our imagination, though, is the real driver.

You can seed your daily meditation with a request for inspiration or just the seed or nuance of an idea. If you are meant to run with it, you will get a message of how to proceed. The message might arrive in the meditation or during the day, often in the most bizarre manner.

9. Saying thank you

When you do spot a sign, get a message, or some good fortune comes your way, it again pays great dividends to say 'Thank you'. You can do this internally and thank your god, your guides, or the universe. You can also express thanks in your deeds and perhaps by performing a random act of kindness to someone else.

Mindful Tasks

What benefits would you like to get from starting a mindfulness practice?

What habits could you break to give you 10 — 20 minutes a day to start meditating?

When can you start?

Part 2

The Illusion of Time

TIME, AS WE KNOW IT, ONLY EXISTS WHEN AN OBSERVER IS PRESENT.

When you are asleep, the clock stops until you wake up.

The concept of time is a good thing, as it allows us to run our modern society. Go back just five hundred years or so and nobody had a watch. Church bells counted time. Even in the nineteenth century, the factory hooter was the main way the workforce got awoken. Wristwatches only became commonplace towards the end of the 1800s.

We count time in strange ways. Minutes and seconds are counted in base 60. Hours in base 12 and 24. Days of the week are counted up to 7. Weeks work in batches of 52. Months have a chronology and counting system that carries no form, and not much function. Yet our current time system allows us to catch a train on time in order, ideally, to get to work on time. We know when it is time to go home and when to switch on the TV to watch our favourite program.

No other animal, or plant, uses it. Dogs know when it's walk time, food time, and sleep time. Plants know when to hibernate and when to blossom. Corals spawn in synchronism with the Full Moon.

The only real time constants are the rotation of the Earth on its axis, the orbit of the Moon around the Earth, and the orbit of the Earth around the Sun. Even these times vary somewhat. Seconds, minutes, hours, weeks, and months are man-made. While they have their uses, we can become governed by them.

As humans, we are indoctrinated from birth with food times, bath times, and sleep times. At school, our curriculum is delivered by a timetable. Old Father time beats a steady clock that counts up (or is that down?) past our 30th, 40th, 50th, and 60th birthdays. Before we know it, it's time to put on our slippers and collect our pension. One day, our time will be up, as time waits for no man, or so it seems. Incidentally, quotes such as these always mention 'man' and it is 'man' that has both created and enslaved us 'in time'.

We take time for granted, yet it is one of the biggest illusions. Time is only linear, and with a forward arrow, if we let it be so. The equations of physics work in both directions.

I am sure this has happened to you. You are driving somewhere, and you think you are going to be late. Yet, somehow, and as if by magic, you get to your end destination exactly on time. With some cunning, you might even manifest a parking space right outside.

Conversely, this also may have happened to you. You have a busy day where nothing goes right. Something makes you late for your first appointment, and this kicks everything out of kilter for the rest of the day.

The key to generating more time is to begin the day with mindful meditation. When we are awake, it is the speed and nature of our thoughts that dictate how we perceive time. We 'speak' internally at much the same speed that we talk out loud. It is this inner dialogue that beats a silent 'clock' inside our brains. When we make our mind go quiet, it slows this clock down.

The speed of our breath affects the speed at which we speak and think. Slow the breath down, and time elongates. This is why meditation works so well, as moderation of the breath is the precursor to entering the trance state. Maintaining the meditative trance state with our eyes open expands time during our waking day.

When we live timefully, we not only get more done with less time, but we also find out that external events seem to happen just at the right time. It is such a joy to live like this that, once you learn how to do it, it is hard to remember what it was like to behave in any other way.

So mindfulness meditation leads to timefulness because it teaches us how to manage our thoughts. As I mentioned, if we are thinking about the past or the future, we will lose focus on the present. This drastically reduces our efficiency.

There is another benefit to entering the meditative state when we are working creatively. As well as elongating time, it prevents our thought forms about others 'leaking out' and potentially being picked up by people who might think to interrupt us. It seems we create an 'interruption barrier'.

I hope you are taking on board that it's a kind of madness not to meditate.

Living Timefully

WHEN WE LIVE TIMEFULLY, WE NOT ONLY GET MORE DONE WITH LESS TIME, BUT WE ALSO FIND OUT THAT EXTERNAL EVENTS SEEM TO HAPPEN JUST AT THE RIGHT TIME.

It is such a joy to live like this that, once you learn how to do it, it is hard to remember what it was like to behave in any other way.

So how do we move from being time poor to being time enriched? Here are nine simple ways to make more from your days:

1. Keep a Diary

It might sound a bit basic but keeping a diary is a great way to manage time, whether it's a paper or electronic version. The reason being is that a diary is a Whole Brain device. In one view, the right brain gets an overall picture of a day, a week, or a month. At the same time, the left brain can focus on the detail.

I even colour-code different types of tasks in my diary so that I can see clearly when I've allocated time to write, to meet clients, to podcast, and to play.

2. Keep Appointments

Once you have a diary with most of your time allocated, it's easier not to be swayed to move it around if something or someone wants to book a meeting when you have something scheduled. In my diary, I have 'meetings' booked with this chapter and all other chapters in my books. If a client booking comes in, I schedule it around my writing time. If I didn't, the books would not get written. Of course, some of us feel more creative in the mornings, and some in the evenings. If you are a writer or an artist, be mindful of the optimum time to block out in your diary to strut your creative stuff.

3. Be On Time

Once you have a diary and a schedule, your side of the bargain is to stick to it. If things slip a little, ask yourself if the time bandit of procrastination is in operation. If you are meeting someone, be respectful of their time and ideally get to the meeting point a few minutes ahead of schedule.

4. Make Creative Dates

Even if you are not a creative by trade and have creative time scheduled, it pays great dividends to have time set aside for your creative side to play.

So, at least each month, if not each week, try and ensure you either engage in some creative activity or see others so involved. You might take up an art class or visit an art gallery. You might learn a musical instrument or go see others playing.

When we do this, we give our left brain a holiday from being 'in time' and it has the effect of slowing time down in general.

5. Be In Time

When you are in a meeting or working on a creative task, or on a creative date, fully immerse yourself. Switch off your phone, don't check emails or social media. Be present and in the present. Honour your time and the time of people you are meeting. If you are engaged creatively, honour the process and the privilege of having the gift of such creative time.

6. Allow Things to Arrive

A shaman once told me that I was trying too hard to make things happen and that, although I was a good manifestor, that more would come my way if I just allowed it. While our brains are engaged thinking about what we want, they are in transmit mode. If we allow our brains to go quiet and our lower mind centres to act as our guides, what we desire will just show up.

7. Roll with the Days

The days of the week are arbitrary, being associated mostly with the names of gods and goddesses, and we can re-allocate them so we can focus on different tasks on different days.

For example, my typical week looks like this:

- Monday = Mends Day = client healing days
- Tuesday = Tools Day = creation of online resources for clients
- Wednesday = Weeds Day = creative unblocking sessions
- Thursday = Surge Day = a day for marketing activities
- Friday = Free Day = a day to be open to anything

I always take weekends off and, on every weekday, I write or create content from around 8:30 am through to 10:30 am irrespective of the focus of that day.

8. Follow the Moon

When projects stretch over a number of days, we can use the Moon Phase to modulate our activities and focus. The New Moon is a great time to kick off a project. From New Moon to Full Moon is the time for project gestation. Full Moon to New Moon is the time to take action. Note that this works either because the Moon affects our consciousness or that thinking before acting is a good strategy in life.

9. A Plan for All Seasons

We can also work to the seasons. Only after publishing my first three books did it occur to me that I started writing them in spring. So, each year, I write my major book then. Autumn is then a good time to launch and reap the harvest. When we manage our time with the natural cycles, it is amazing how we can get more done in less of it.

Timeful Tasks

What would you do if you had more time?

Where are your time leaks?

How are you being creatively uncreative?

Part 3

Being Kind to Yourself

IN THE SAME WAY THAT THE PRACTICE OF
MINDFULNESS LEADS US NATURALLY INTO A STATE
OF TIMEFULNESS, TIMEFULNESS NATURALLY
LEADS US TO BEING ABLE TO DEMONSTRATE
KINDFULNESS.

This, of course, is the point of the title of this book.

When we get more things done in less time, this gives us more time not only to be kind to others but to be kind to ourselves.

I was brought up to 'do for others' ahead of serving my own needs. On the surface this is a kind way to be but it can produce adverse and undesirable side effects. Firstly, it can be the seed of lack of self-worth. Secondly, we can undermine our talents and prevent ourselves from shining our true light.

If you are unfortunate enough to be in an aeroplane that depressurises, you are told to don your oxygen mask first, so you are better placed to assist others.
In the same way that nobody can eat, think, or love for you, nobody else can breathe for you.

When it comes to being kind to others, it is crucial you are kind to yourself first.

As an example of this, a few years back, I got into a pattern of helping other clients write their books ahead of writing my own. I had a script running in my head that said, 'It doesn't matter if one of my books doesn't become a bestseller so long as, with my help, one of my clients has a bestselling book.'

One day it dawned on me that this was a dumb strategy. The very experience of producing a bestselling book is of infinite benefit that can be shared with my clients. Incidentally, what was really occurring was that I was being creatively uncreative and using clients as the excuse for not shining my own light.

This was an unkindness to me (and potential readers of this and my other books) masquerading behind the veneer of being kind to others first.

So, being kind to yourself starts by giving yourself some 'me time'. Morning meditation is a great way to begin, as it impacts upon nobody and generates such benefit for everyone, starting with us. The next step is to allow yourself time to pick up new skills and develop your promise.

New knowledge leads to new thoughts and opens new doors to new possibilities.

The whole process is, of course, cyclical. As you become more capable of getting more done, it can lead to more money coming your way from your employment. If, like me, you are self-employed, getting more done in less time means you can be kinder to yourself about the hours you work and the nature of your work.

I don't work weekends, and in the week I don't work at all because I love what I do so much that it's hard to classify it as 'work'. Of course, with Catholic guilt never far from my shoulder, I give myself a harder time than I ought, and I am probably my own worst critic. When I am 'working', as I am now as I write these words, I am diligent in my approach and mindful of the words I string together.

We can be kind to ourselves in myriads of ways. I reward myself at the end of writing a chapter with a cup of tea and the occasional biscuit (or cookie). I am generally kind to my digestive system and eat quite healthily. I am not an ascetic, though, and treat myself to a glass of wine and love a pint or two of 'warm beer'.

I also believe that the state of mind we are in when we eat or drink something has a huge bearing on how harmful, or good, it is for us. I am sharing this sentiment as a kindness to those who read too much into newspaper headlines about the latest report into what makes us ill. Our minds are by far the biggest influencers when it comes down to causes of dis-ease— and it is our state of mind that encourages good health and fosters well-being.

If we should become ill, the biggest kindness we can bestow on ourselves is to be mindful of our thoughts and our lifestyle. I am not advocating that you don't see a doctor or take a pill, but to see dis-ease as a gift and a sign that something is out of kilter in your life.

Perhaps such illness is just a sign that we need to be kinder to ourselves, and that it's time to treat ourselves to a holiday.

Being Kind to Others

PERHAPS COUNTER-INTUITIVELY, THEN, BEING KIND TO OURSELVES FIRST PUTS US INTO A MUCH BETTER AND STRONGER POSITION WHEN IT COMES TO HELPING OTHERS.

People can see we are in good shape and being productive and, without having to brag about it, our state of being sets up well so that we can act as a guide and role model for others. Also, when we have more time on our hands, we are in a much better position to be kinder to others.

By far and away my favourite acts of kindness are the ones that are random. They can be as simple as opening a door for a stranger or letting a car out in traffic. One I use on new social media contacts whose profiles I find intriguing goes down particularly well and has often been copied.

I ask, 'Thanks for connecting so-and-so ... what can I do for you that will take me no more than a minute but that will really make your day?'

What is, perhaps, bizarre is that the most common response is simply my permission for the new contact to be able to use this question on others. My response to them takes just a few seconds, of course.

With random acts of kindness, we should be mindful of a few caveats. Firstly, they should, of course, be random and not premeditated. Secondly, do not expect those you bestow the kindness on to be where kindness comes back to you. Thirdly, when any such kindnesses are bestowed on you, be thankful and accept them with grace.

Such a strategy spreads, and each person you are kind to will inevitably pass it on. When I let a car out in traffic, so it is now in front of me, I notice how they do the same to others in front of them. While this might slow me down a bit more, the world as a whole moves a little faster. What goes around comes around. We will all get there much faster together in the end.

It is not just people we should be kind to but all life forms on the planet. Whether you eat meat or are vegetarian or pescatarian, something has given up its life in order to give you sustenance. Be mindful and thankful of that.

Our pets have feelings too, even fish, and especially cats, dogs, and budgies. They also pick up on our moods, so we should be mindful of how we are feeling when we are around them.

It might sound somewhat esoteric but nature, too, likes to be appreciated.

Plants and trees have a level of consciousness (and speed of time) that is different to ours. It is well documented, though, that plant life blossoms in a kind and loving environment. Hug a tree today and you'll get a hug back from someone else, even if metaphorically.

The Earth, too, as do all planets and stars, has awareness. Our Mother Earth works from a position of unconditional love for us. The gravity that sticks us to the planet is an expression of that love. Gravity also holds an atmosphere for us to breathe and water for us to drink. It pulls roots of plants into the soil that feeds them and, ultimately, us. The constant spin and orbit of the planet keeps everything alive and in motion. It is this, combined with the Sun's rays, which powers and enables all life. We should be constantly mindful and thankful of this.

Being thankful to the Earth takes two main forms.

Firstly, we should ensure we leave the planet in a better state than when we arrived upon it. This starts with small acts like not dropping litter and picking it up if others have left a trail. We should also be mindful of the energy we consume. If you can go 'eco' and energy neutral in your home, hats off to you. If not, just switching off electrical devices that you are not using will help. Putting a jumper on before firing up your central heating system will save you money and the planet energy.

Secondly, like plants, the Earth likes to be appreciated and loved back in return.

You can express your love for the planet in simple ways. When out in nature, or even when watching a nature or wildlife documentary, appreciate and be in awe of the beauty the Earth holds and sustains on her surface.

Let me share a simple mindful, meditative technique you can practice when out in nature in the daytime. It can be done at night too, looking at the Moon and stars.

Stand facing the Sun. If it's cloudy, work out where the Sun is approximately. Close your eyes if it's sunny.

Stand with your legs slightly apart and, if you are not shy or no one is looking, with your arms out to your side and your hands splayed and facing the Sun.

Allow the sunlight to enter your body at your Third Eye—in between your eyebrows.

Route the sunlight down your spine into your legs and allow it to enter the Earth through your feet.

Be mindful and thankful to the Sun as being the Life-Giver, who has gifted you this time on this special planet.

Be mindful and thankful to the Earth as being your Life-Sustainer while you are here.

Be mindful that the Sun and the Earth have planned this moment for billions of years.

You are their creation and expression of self-awareness, born of stardust.

Go forth about your days being mindful, timeful, and kindful.

Living Kindfully

WHEN WE LIVE KINDFULLY, WE BECOME
ATTRACTIVE IN ALL SENSES OF THE WORD.

Being kind-full is 'nicely infectious'. People you are
kind to become kind to others—and back to you. We
become a true force to be reckoned with, and people
take notice and want some of whatever it is we seem to
have.

So, how do you live a kind-full existence? Here are
nine simple, kindful exercises:

1. Sweet Dreams

The point between being asleep and being awake is
called the hypnopompic time. It is a time when we can
best remember our dreams. Awaken slowly and allow
them to percolate into your consciousness. Ask if there
is a message within them that can help you in the day
ahead.

2. Awaken with Purpose

As you start your day, just muse on what would be the most fantastic outcome for the day ahead. If any challenges face you, just imagine how you will feel when you tackle them with aplomb. Ask yourself what new serendipities might appear that will make the day ahead magical and special.

3. Make Someone's Day

As you go about your day, be mindful that you can become the serendipity someone else might be looking for in their day. Imagine how this person would feel when you make their day. Imagine how proud you will feel when you have a positive impact on someone else's life.

4. Turning Points

Today, like all days, holds the potential to become a turning point. Someone or something might show up that will change your world. Your job is to notice and pay attention for when they occur. At the same time, be open to the possibility that you may create and provide a turning point for someone else.

5. Leave a Breadcrumb Trail

Be mindful each day that you are laying down memories for the future. As you become the change you would like to see in the world, it's important you remember how you got there.

Keeping a journal or writing a blog is a great way to leave a trail that others can follow, and that reminds you of your path of evolution.

6. Shine Your Light

Your breadcrumb trail will only be useful to others if they can find it. A kindful way to show others what you have learned is to create content others can consume and access. These days, as publishing has become easy and democratised, this may be a book like this, or a blog or a podcast or YouTube channel. You can equally shine your light by example and just by showing up in the world.

7. End Endarkenment

One of the illusions of our existence is that life is intrinsically hard and that the world is out to get us. Nothing is further from the truth. The Universe is a kind and benevolent place. If it weren't, we wouldn't even be here to experience it. Pass this message on and encourage all you come across to see their glass as being half full rather than being half empty. Then get them to fill their glass to the brim, so it is overflowing.

8. Slow and Steady Wins the Race

When we learn to be timeful, we will get more done in less time. This can create a backlash of pressure to rush projects through. See this time-bending ability as a gift, not a burden.

Use the extra time created to finesse your output and to be mindful and timeful of when you deliver. You will be being kindful to yourself and others by not only making time but also taking your time.

9. Sleeping Mindfully

The point between being awake and being asleep is called the hypnagogic time. This is the perfect point in the day to bestow one last kindfulness on yourself. As you drift off, muse on the highlights and serendipities of the day. Be thankful for those that came your way. Be thankful, too, for any challenges and learnings. Muse on what would make the following day ahead even more magical. Ask for guidance in your dreams. Sleep tight.

Kindful Tasks

How can you be kinder to yourself?

What kindnesses can you bestow on others today?

How can you be kinder to the planet?

what's next?

THIS BOOK IS ACCOMPANIED BY THREE
MEDITATIVE VISUALISATIONS TO HELP YOU
EXPERIENCE THE STATE OF 'MIND-FULL-NESS'
AND 'TIME-FULL-NESS'. THERE'S ALSO A BONUS
SHORT STORY ON THE POWER OF RANDOM ACTS
OF 'KINDFULNESS'.

Meditation 1: 10 Minutes of Mindfulness

This meditation takes just 10 minutes to listen to,
ideally in the morning, and is the perfect tonic to set
you up for the most amazing day ahead.

Meditation 2: Be Calm

This visualisation takes you through the most common ways to make your mind go quiet—by meditating on a mantra, on the breath, and on thought itself.

Meditation 3: Noticing Time

This sample visualisation, from my Living Timefully program, demonstrates how the passage of time is subjective.

Use the code MTK100 on checkout to get these visualisations for free here:

http://www.tomevans.co/10-minutes-of-mindfulness/

And, if you want to bag some extra karma points, I would be eternally grateful if you left a review of this book on Amazon. What goes around comes around!

Mindful Timeful Kindful in Practice

THE BEST WAY TO BE MINDFUL TIMEFUL AND KINDFUL IS TO LIVE IT AND BREATHE IT.

It only takes a relatively short amount of time to turn our world upon its head. The wiring between our neurons in our brains is 'plastic' and we can change how our neurons wire and fire together in an instant.

When we then practice something for only 21 days, it becomes hard-wired into our neurology and we become able to do it without thinking about it consciously. It becomes engrained in our being

So for the next 21 days, use this book, or a notepad to keep a journal. If you miss a day, don't fret about it. If you are buzzing after just a week, just live it and don't waste too much time writing it down. If you want to keep it going longer than 21 days, just keep going. If you think of other things you would like to keep a journal on, add those into the mix too.

As you get results from this simple exercise, have fun with it. Make your 'mindfulnesses' and 'kindfulnesses' bigger and bolder. You will notice, as a result, how the 'timefulnesses' increase in both frequency and scale.

Note that you can use this journalling for either your personal or business life—or both. Here's what to record in your journal:

Mindfulnesses

Make a note of things that are on your mind that you would like to get off it. This might be events or people you would like out of your life. They may be happenings you would like in your world, such as your goals and dreams.

Timefulnesses

Make a note of serendipities and good fortune that visits your door each day, especially those that come along when you are least expecting them.

Kindfulnesses

When you are kind to either yourself or someone else, jot it down. Make a note, too, if someone is unexpectedly kind to you.

Day 1

Mindfulnesses

_____

_____

_____

_____

Timefulnesses

_____

_____

_____

_____

Kindfulnesses

_____

_____

_____

_____

Day 2

Mindfulnesses

_____

_____

_____

_____

Timefulnesses

_____

_____

_____

Kindfulnesses

_____

_____

_____

_____

Day 3

Mindfulnesses

Timefulnesses

Kindfulnesses

Day 4

Mindfulnesses

_____

_____

_____

_____

Timefulnesses

_____

_____

_____

Kindfulnesses

_____

_____

_____

_____

Day 5

Mindfulnesses

Timefulnesses

Kindfulnesses

Day 6

Mindfulnesses

Timefulnesses

Kindfulnesses

Day 7

Mindfulnesses

_____

_____

_____

_____

Timefulnesses

_____

_____

_____

Kindfulnesses

_____

_____

_____

_____

Day 8

Mindfulnesses

_____

_____

_____

_____

Timefulnesses

_____

_____

_____

_____

Kindfulnesses

_____

_____

_____

_____

Day 9

Mindfulnesses

Timefulnesses

Kindfulnesses

Day 10

Mindfulnesses

Timefulnesses

Kindfulnesses

Day 11

Mindfulnesses

_____

_____

_____

_____

Timefulnesses

_____

_____

_____

Kindfulnesses

_____

_____

_____

_____

Day 12

Mindfulnesses

Timefulnesses

Kindfulnesses

Day 13

Mindfulnesses

_____

_____

_____

_____

Timefulnesses

_____

_____

_____

Kindfulnesses

_____

_____

_____

_____

Day 14

Mindfulnesses

_____

_____

_____

_____

Timefulnesses

_____

_____

_____

_____

Kindfulnesses

_____

_____

_____

_____

Day 15

Mindfulnesses

_____

_____

_____

_____

Timefulnesses

_____

_____

_____

_____

Kindfulnesses

_____

_____

_____

_____

Day 16

Mindfulnesses

Timefulnesses

Kindfulnesses

Day 17

Mindfulnesses

Timefulnesses

Kindfulnesses

Day 18

Mindfulnesses

_____

_____

_____

_____

Timefulnesses

_____

_____

_____

Kindfulnesses

_____

_____

_____

_____

Day 19

Mindfulnesses

Timefulnesses

Kindfulnesses

Day 20

Mindfulnesses

_____

_____

_____

_____

Timefulnesses

_____

_____

_____

Kindfulnesses

_____

_____

_____

_____

Day 21

Mindfulnesses

Timefulnesses

Kindfulnesses

Tomography

TOM EVANS IS AN EX-BBC TV ENGINEER WHO BECAME AN AUTHOR BY ACCIDENT IN HIS MID-40S, AFTER DISCOVERING HOW TO MEDITATE.

These days, his writing has become a full-time occupation, and he is also the host of the popular podcast, The Zone Show.

His clients refer to him with many monikers such as thebookwright, the wizard of lightbulb moments, and temporal alchemist.

From Tom's perspective, he still doesn't know what he wants to be when he grows up.

Find out more at www.tomevans.co

Follow him on Twitter at www.twitter.com/thebookwright

Bibliography

Non-fiction Titles

Blocks
The Art and Science of Light Bulb Moments
Flavours of Thought
Planes of Being
The Zone
This We Know
This We Are
New Magic for a New Era

Short Stories

One Hundred Years of Ermintrude
Soulwave
The Germinatrix

Acknowledgements

AS WITH ALL PROJECTS, THIS SERIES OF BOOKS WOULD NOT HAPPEN IF IT WASN'T FOR SEEDS AND ASSISTANCE PROVIDED BY OTHER PEOPLE.

So, big thanks to TheCreativePenn, Joanna Penn, for giving me the idea for creating a series of books that is topical, relevant, and enlightening.

Thanks to Denise Harris-Heigho and Jackie Walker for being the best sounding boards an author could ever have.

Thanks to Harmony Kent for massaging my words into something that makes sense.

Thanks to Steve Palfreyman for helping me get all the ducks in a row.

Thanks to Tina Fotherby for helping me shine my light.

Thanks to the big heart that is Doug New.